Want support along the way?

Click on

http://astotz.com/deming-member

and join our community.

When you join you can:
Ask questions about your specific case
Get access to answers to frequently asked questions
Join the discussion on each major topic in this book

Also by Andrew Stotz
You Won't Get Rich in the Stock Market
… Until You Change the Way You Think About It

Transform Your Business with Dr. Deming's 14 Points

Andrew Stotz

A Note to the Reader

This book is written and designed to provide accurate and
authoritative information on the subject of the teaching of Dr.
Deming as understood by the author. The contents of this book
are intended as a general guide on the topics covered in it. The
book is sold with the understanding that neither the Author nor
the Publisher is engaged in rendering legal, consulting,
accounting or other professional services by publishing this
book.

As of the date of publishing, all contents in the book, such as
information, data, and web links are accurate and up to date to
the best knowledge of the Author and Publisher. The Author
and Publisher cannot be held responsible for any inaccuracies.
The Author and the Publisher specifically deny responsibility for
any liability, loss or risk that may be suffered as a consequence
of, indirectly or directly, applying any of the ideas contained in
this book.

DEDICATION

Thanks to my Mom and Dad, who never gave up on me.

CONTENTS

ACKNOWLEDGMENTS

I would like to thank Kelly Allan, John Hunter and Kevin Cahill of the Deming Institute for their value feedback. Further thanks go to Dr. Nabil Tamimi of University of Scranton and Dr. Rajiv Mehta of New Jersey Institute of Technology for their valuable input.
And most importantly, thanks to Dr. W. Edwards Deming for delivering his energy and passion to me. What I learned in my very short times listening to him changed my life forever. Finally, thanks to my CoffeeWORKS business partner and lifelong friend, Dale Lee. We discovered the teachings of Dr. Deming in our youth and have built a business and our lives around his principles.

INTRODUCTION

This book started as an internal training guide at my company, CoffeeWORKS Co., Ltd. in Bangkok, Thailand.

My business partner, Dale Lee, and I had absorbed the teachings of Dr. W. Edwards Deming at a young age, but the trouble we encountered was how to effectively communicate to our staff what Dr. Deming taught. Since they are all non-native speakers of English, our staff rightfully complained that his teachings were difficult to understand.

So I went about rereading Dr. Deming's book, *Out of the Crisis* (my cherished copy signed by the author), and decided that the most concrete thing we could bring to our team was his 14 Points for Management. From there I started taking notes, trying to come up with simpler, clearer ways to explain the profound and groundbreaking concepts that Dr. Deming developed.

This book was built on those notes, and all the ideas contained here originate from Dr. Deming. The little value that I added was to simplify and shorten his message to make it digestible for those who would otherwise not consider diving into his original material.

Additional resources:
Andrew: http://youtu.be/Hy_ida-K5Yo

1 CREATE CONSTANCY OF PURPOSE

Create constancy of purpose toward improvement of products and services, with the aim of becoming competitive, staying in business, and providing jobs.

Top management's job is to create a clear long-term vision.

Long-term "constancy of purpose" is a top management duty. In fact, Deming considers it management's number one priority. Unlike other management thinkers, Deming highlights that it is not the employees' duty to set the long-term direction of the firm. If a company gets off-track from that purpose, management must take appropriate action immediately. Clear, long-term aims lead to clear policies, reasonable goals and resourcing plans. This makes it easy to communicate to workers what is happening within the company, which leads to a higher level of morale and lower staff turnover.

Create stability and longevity – lasting quality improvements take time.

The long term is important and should serve as the focus for changes. Target the future, become more competitive, grow, and provide for long-term needs rather than short-term profits. Having a long-term purpose creates company conditions of stability and longevity, and a time frame during which continuous improvement is realistic. Investment in process quality and product innovation leads to rewards in the future.

Find balance between day-to-day problems and the long-term view, but bear in mind that managers striving for long-term aims must not ignore day-to-day problems. Short-term survival depends on solving these problems, but Deming warns that a balance between short- and long-term goals should be found at all levels of the organization.

Many companies spend time dealing with regular challenges – such as quarterly dividends, yearly profit-sharing checks, etc. – instead of the long-term objectives of remaining in business, flourishing, and developing. Short-term targets are typically the opposite of what should be long-term focused ambitions.

Replace short-term reaction with long-term planning and innovation.

Set a path designed to drive the firm toward product and service improvement. But remember that overcoming future problems will require focus and consistent, sustained purpose. Accept responsibility for innovating. Managers should replace short-term reactions to day-to-day problems with long-term planning. But this doesn't mean that we should disregard short-term goals. Stability is needed for both within the business.

Apply lessons from the past and present in training and education.

Managers must look at past barriers to progress, and identify existing and potential problems. They can then begin to plan and assign resources for training and education, and make risk analyses and contingency plans. By carrying out this strategy, a company can steadily upgrade its services.

Make innovation, education, and continuous improvement company-wide.

Innovation must not be a separate function of a business; rather, it should be an unbroken activity throughout the organization. Management must assign resources into research and education. There must be a focus on continually improving product design and service.

Lead and support employees to continuously improve quality. The task of management must change from giving orders, punishments, and rewards, to leading and supporting the workers to enhance quality. For workers to keep learning about the processes they work in, they need training; to generate ways of improving, they need education. Management must help employees see that change is possible, and that management is committed to developing improved systems and helping employees learn.

Assess how well your company is applying the 14 Points

In 1995, Nabil Tamimi, Mark Gershon, and Steven Currall wrote an academic paper to identify operational measures which could be used to assess the implementation of Dr. Deming's 14 Points in an organization. Their 50 question survey is an excellent resource for self-assessment of implementation. In 2011, Caroline Fisher, Cassandra Elrod and Rajiv Mehta extended this study making some minor modifications. The survey can be done with managers at the business-unit level, but can also be asked of all staff. So, to end each chapter I present the survey that represents each point.

How the survey works:

Respondents should be asked to rank each statement on a five-point scale starting with 0 "not at all true"; 1 "slightly true"; 2 "somewhat true", 3 "mostly true"; and ending with 4, "completely true".

These are the sources I used for the assessments:

Tamimi, N. (1995). An empirical investigation of critical TQM factors using exploratory factor analysis.

International Journal of Production Research, 33 (11), 3041–3051.

Tamimi, N., Gershon, M., & Currall, S. C. (1995). Assessing the psychometric properties of Deming's 14 Principles. Quality Management Journal, Spring, 38–52.

Tamimi, N., & Sebastianelli R. (1996). How firms define and measure quality.

Production and Inventory Management Journal, 37 (3), 34–39.

Caroline M. Fisher, Cassandra C. Elrod, Rajiv Mehta, (2011) "A replication to validate and improve a measurement instrument for Deming's 14 Points", International Journal of Quality & Reliability Management, Vol. 28 Iss: 3, pp.328 – 358.

ASSESSMENT: Rate how well your company is...

1. Creating constancy of purpose

The following statements can help to assess the degree to which this one of Dr. Deming's 14 Points is being implemented. Respondents should rank each statement on a five point scale starting with 0 "not at all true"; 1 "slightly true"; 2 "somewhat true", 3 "mostly true"; and ending with 4, "completely true".

Questions:

1. Top management makes long-term plans.
2. Top management provides for research and development.
3. Top management provides for new technology.
4. Top management promotes employee training/education.

Commentary On Chapter 1

Stotz: One of the most important things I learned from my studies with Dr. Deming was to move away from a quarterly earnings focus. I've studied finance and worked in finance all my career, and it's natural in the world of finance to think about quarterly results. But what Dr. Deming taught was to focus on the long-term—to develop a clear, long-term vision for the company; to communicate that long-term vision to the staff, and [to] make sure that the staff internalizes that vision. And, most importantly, top management should not change the long-term vision, but instead keep the organization focused on it.

Deming: The second deadly disease is emphasis on short-term profits, short-term thinking, and dividends, no matter what! Creative accounting, shipping stuff out, no matter what. Make it look good … devastating to long-term planning, for the plan to stay in business, through improvement of quality, of product and service. They cannot live together.

American management has worshipped the quarterly dividend. They're rated on − "raise the company's stock", anything to raise the price of the company's stock, acquisition, creative accounting.

There's a better way, better way to protect investment, and that is with plans that will keep the company in business and which will provide jobs and work …

Video resources:
   Andrew: http://youtu.be/LXuaRF_-xvs
   Dr. Deming: http://youtu.be/fW4qmMnbkhA

2 ADOPT THE NEW PHILOSOPHY

Adopt the new philosophy. In this new economic age, managers must rise to the challenge, learn their responsibilities, and take them on.

Managers must drive transformation.

They can no longer tolerate the standard acceptance of errors; a good manager must require transformation. Businesses cannot survive today with commonly accepted problems such as defects, workers who do not understand the job and fear asking questions, and the failure of managers to understand internal problems.

It is the managers' duty to sense and find solutions for the flaws existing in the system.

Quality is not a cost-adding element of a product. Many organizations think that quality increases budget, and that to meet this increase, someone (i.e., customers or company) has to pay for it. They believe that if they don't charge more, they cannot bear higher quality. Top management must begin to believe that all employees can find ways to promote quality and efficiency, improve all aspects of the system, and promote excellence and personal accountability.

Employees – with management's support – should adopt a new work philosophy, meeting in "quality circles" (volunteer groups of workers who are trained to identify, analyze, and solve work-related problems and present their solutions to management) to continuously improve. This creates a "continuous learning environment". The common thread in adopting this new philosophy is meeting the needs of those who pay for and use the services provided by the organization, the customers.

Always improve and upgrade; stay focused on customer needs.

The company must adopt a philosophy of endless improvement, actively sensing customers' expectations and helping the company to fulfill them. Management must play the role of leaders, rather than "managers" or followers. Following a philosophy means incorporating it into the organization's journey. Companies need to convert into "learning systems".

Dr. Deming once said, "Effort put in to improve the process increases the uniformity of output (e.g., consistency of service) and cuts waste of manpower." Managers should opt for the new philosophy rather than assuming that the workforce will do so. Their primary principles must be visible through their interactions with teams and associates. Management is only a fragment of an organization, so adoption of the philosophy will require a wholesale acceptance by workers as well.

Major change comes when we look at customers, not competitors.

When management looks forward – not at competitors, but at customers – that will be the moment of major change. Management must confront weak performance and demonstrate the ability to handle distracting conflicts. Management should help employees to understand their responsibility to contribute to customer satisfaction and the profitability of the business. Employees should feel encouraged to look for occasions to improve their work procedures, process, and environment.

If we are adopting this new philosophy, we can no longer allow:

Management to not be involved in the company

- Employees on the job not understanding their job responsibility
- Wrongdoing in (and damage to) the firm
- Outdated ways of training
- Sparse and inefficient instruction
- Commonly accepted frequency of errors
- Reworking imperfect products

ASSESSMENT: Rate how well your company is...

2. Adopting the new philosophy

The following statements can help to assess the degree to which this one of Dr. Deming's 14 Points is being implemented. Respondents should rank each statement on a five point scale starting with 0 "not at all true"; 1 "slightly true"; 2 "somewhat true", 3 "mostly true"; and ending with 4, "completely true".

Questions:

1. Top management is committed to quality improvement as a way to increase profits.
2. Top management is committed to setting objectives for quality improvement.
3. Top management is committed to setting continuous quality enhancement as a primary goal.

Commentary on Chapter 2

Stotz: When I studied my MBA, what I learned was how to manage and administer a business. And, when I started my career at Pepsi in Los Angeles, it was, in fact, my job to supervise and manage teams of workers. As I moved up in my career—and later when we started our company, CoffeeWORKS, in Thailand in 1995—I started to better understand what Dr. Deming had taught about the difference between leading and managing. Leading is about setting the vision, about directing the focus of the company, and keeping that focus on the customer; on the customer's needs, wants and pressures. When I attended my first Deming seminar in 1989, Dr. Deming's thinking started pushing me to another level, to the idea that it was up to me to direct the efforts of my team toward a long-term goal. It was not my job to fight with other departments to best represent my team. Rather, it was my job to try to work together with other departments to achieve our long-term goals.

I have heard it said that Dr. Deming was overly focused on quality, but I remember clearly him saying that a company could build an amazing quality system and still go out of business if that quality system was not focused on the needs of the customers.

Deming: The annual system of rating salaried people, known also as merit system, annual appraisal of performance, annual rating of performance, known also under the name "management by objective". Someone in Germany called it "management by fear", which is still better.

Pay for merit, pay for what you get, reward performance, sounds great. It can't be done.

Unfortunately, it cannot be done on short range. After 10 years, perhaps, 20 years, yes. But Americans have, somehow become obsessed, from many years back and nobody knows where it originated, that everybody must be appraised.

Now, the effect is devastating. People have to have something to show, something to count. In other words, the system, merit system nourishes short-term performance and annihilates long-term planning. It annihilates teamwork. People cannot work together. To get a promotion, you have to get ahead. By working with a team, you help other people. You may help yourself equally, but you don't get ahead. By being equal, you get ahead by being ahead, produce something more, have more to show, more to count.

Teamwork means – work together, hear everybody's ideas, fill in for other people's weaknesses, acknowledge their strengths, and work together.

It's impossible under the merit rating and review of performance. People are afraid. They're in fear. They work in fear. They cannot contribute to the company as they would wish to contribute.

Video resources:
Andrew: http://youtu.be/RMVzOzkRAA8
Dr. Deming: http://youtu.be/4P6Tq2XhLMc

3 END DEPENDENCE ON QUALITY INSPECTIONS

Cease dependence on inspection to achieve quality. Eliminate the need for mass inspection by building quality into the product from the start. Management should shift its focus to creating and continually improving systems so that they consistently produce the desired results.

Achieve quality output by starting at the beginning of the process.

Quality checks at the end of the production line do not achieve excellence. It is far better to work together to improve design and development at the beginning of the process. Inspections after manufacturing come too late in the process and cost too much in time, money, effort, and morale. Inspections fail for a number of reasons: Some defects always get through, some good products may be misclassified as bad, and even 200% inspection doesn't work, as inspectors sometimes fail to agree with each other.

Detection of defects is therefore not a viable competitive strategy. Instead, prevent defects by using process feedback and customer feedback. Engaging in mass inspection does not generate quality – bulk examination is expensive and useless. The data collected would be better used to improve process control.

Use inspection for feedback during production.

Old thinking says inspection stops bad quality. The old way was for companies to create the product first, then inspect for defects. By then, it's too late! Spot the defect after production, and you have to return it to be corrected or discard it. It is usually a lot harder to fix a product than it is to build quality into the product at the beginning.

But that does not mean we eliminate all inspection. We can use inspection to judge progress – and not leave it to production's final stages. It is often too late to react to product quality when it has reached a customer's hands. During inspection, we waste too much time defining what is and isn't good, then confirming to see if and why the parameters were met or unmet. We look for insignificant issues, leaving behind important areas – never exactly sure, always modifying, and doing more harm than good.

To prevent all of this, we need to support and offer technical reviews, walk-throughs and inspections as gentle methods to reach quality throughout the development phase. Inspection should be used as an information-gathering tool to understand the state of the process, not as a means of "assuring" quality or accusing workers of poor performance.

Regulate processes, not outcomes.

Most organizations focus on regulating the outcome rather than the process, where the root of the problem usually lies. Solving this root problem can prevent complaints from arising. When a company manages the outcome, it becomes focused on keeping customers satisfied. When it manages the process, it is much better, because customers will experience the improvements, and then talk about how satisfied they are. The real measure of service quality comes when the customers are satisfied and tell others about their satisfaction with the product and service.

Service quality is a core reason that a company retains customers and attracts new ones. Make the entire company passionate about excellence, and treat quality as a tangible asset. Rather than leaving the problems for someone else down the production line, employees must care for their work. Quality has to be designed and built into the product – it cannot be inspected into it. Sometimes it is only the workers on the production line who can see when designs and work processes don't make sense, and they need to be supported and allowed to speak up. Also remember that the quality of back office, sales, software, and service activities are also part of the process. Make sure to gather statistical data on these areas.

Enhance production methods. Prevent problems rather than trying to fix those that have already occurred. Project management and work processes need constant improvements built into them to minimize quality problems. The intention of inspection is not to send the product for rework, because that raises costs without adding value.

Boost knowledge of processes and methods.

Recognize what flaws are built-in to the process, and work to reduce their impact. Work continuously to design error-free processes. Upgrade all systems. The urgency for inspection will decrease if quality issues are stopped in the beginning stages.

ASSESSMENT: Rate how well your company is...

3. Ending reliance on mass inspection

The following statements can help to assess the degree to which this one of Dr. Deming's 14 Points is being implemented. Respondents should rank each statement on a five point scale starting with 0 "not at all true"; 1 "slightly true"; 2 "somewhat true", 3 "mostly true"; and ending with 4, "completely true".

Questions:

1. Suppliers use statistical quality control techniques.

2. Statistical quality control techniques are used to minimize reliance on mass inspection.

3. Top management supports the belief that quality must be "built into" the product, not "inspected into" it.

Commentary on Chapter 3

Stotz: Dr. Deming taught me to focus on the beginning of any process. If the beginning is poorly constructed, problems multiply exponentially as you move down the process. I also learned that every business is exactly that: a process—a series of activities (like links in a chain) that must work together to create a final outcome for the customer. In this sense, every business is the same—it is simply a series of activities that come together to deliver value to the customer.

The job of management is first to understand that we are dealing with a system, not a single activity; and then to focus the management team on this system, rather than each manager only focusing on his area. We do this within CoffeeWORKS by having weekly management team meetings, bringing together managers of each of the areas to sort through and discuss the problems and difficulties they are each facing. The key is not to allow any one manager to make their area great at the expense of another. Rather, the challenge is to make all great at the same time.

To give an example about focusing on activities rather than outcomes, we focus our sales team not on numerical sales targets but rather on how many cold calls they've made, how many networking events they have attended, how many follow-ups they have made with prior contacts or how we can improve the sales process. Dr. Deming taught me to trust that if we get these inputs or activities right, then the right outcomes or results will follow. Without a proper focus on activities, you end up threatening salespeople with sales targets, and both parties end up frustrated.

When I first learned of Dr. Deming, I was living in Los Angeles. My roommate was Dale Lee, my childhood friend from our hometown of Hudson, Ohio. I came back from my first Deming seminar filled with excitement to share what I had learned, and Dale was really interested in this non-conventional way of thinking. At the time, we would sit down and read passages from Dr. Deming's book, Out of the Crisis, and then discuss it. Little did we know at the time that we would have the chance to implement his teachings as co-owners of a coffee factory in Thailand.

Deming: That's a path toward destruction because they're not studying the system. They're managing outcomes, managing defects instead of looking at the system that produced the defects.

Video resources:
Andrew: http://youtu.be/jOs0GUki2r8
Dr. Deming: http://youtu.be/-wkv4vEYKr4

4 STOP AWARDING BUSINESS TO SUPPLIERS ON THE BASIS OF PRICE

End the practice of awarding business based on the price tag. Instead, minimize total cost. Move toward a single supplier for any one item, and create a long-term relationship built on loyalty and trust.

Minimize total cost, not just initial cost.

Awarding business on quality, value, speed, and a long-term relationship will decrease total costs, which should be management's focus. Many companies award deals to the lowest bidder, but low bids do not promise quality. Unless quality is delivered, the effective cost per unit is much greater when flaws are factored in.

What is important to a business is the total cost of the product/service and not the cost of individual elements. A company could buy any component of a production process at a lower cost, but doing so may interfere with the ability to deliver long-term quality.

A multiple-supplier system has long been used for security against supply chain disruptions (such as natural disasters) and to force suppliers to compete on price. But such continuous change of suppliers based on price increases fluctuations in the material supplied to production, since each supplier's procedures are different. The additional variation caused by swapping from one supplier to another needs to be seen as a problem that a business brings upon itself.

A company should try to work with one supplier to lower total cost over time.

Buying a low-priced product from a supplier who won't work to improve it will prove far more costly than paying a little extra for a supplier who commits to continuous improvement. Costs of repairs and making do with lesser products should be considered along with direct costs of raw material before making purchasing selections. Purchasing staff may not always see these hidden costs and only focus on the lowest cost option.

Most importantly, it is top management's responsibility to make sure that all staff are encouraged to speak up, to make sure that total cost and total quality are not disrupted by one individual going for the lowest cost on a particular part.

Evaluate suppliers by meaningful quality measures, along with price.

If you want to meet customers' needs in the long term, you need suppliers who are consistent and trustworthy. Suppliers are more likely to invest in improving quality when they have a good, long-term relationship with you, and are free from the constant trouble of someone underbidding to steal their business.

Nurture relationships; set up mutual trust and understanding between purchaser and seller, make them feel like associates – this can advance your business tremendously. Five suppliers for one part usually mean five times the amount of frustration, resulting in reduced productivity and efficiency.

Let suppliers compete not on price, but on qualifications that have real meaning. Let them prove that their management is using some of Deming's 14 points — especially in improvement of their work processes.

A single supplier relationship allows for easy adjustment to customers' needs.

A long-term link between buyer and vendor is vital for a perfect economy. A buyer can never be innovative and prosper economically in his production processes when he strives for short-term business with a vendor. Build a relationship built on mutual trust, and make your suppliers feel like associates — this can advance your business tremendously. In a single-supplier relationship, both parties can easily adjust to each other's changing needs.

Consumer and supplier function together to create a system for joint gain and happiness, working as friends rather than enemies. The security of the long-term relationship encourages partnership between customers and supplier, and this allows the supplier to take more risks to innovate.

Reducing the number of suppliers ultimately reduces variation in business, which, in turn, lowers total cost.

The objective is a customer-supplier relationship and the application of a cooperation-based "win-win" philosophy. Price alone becomes meaningless as the focus changes from the lowest initial cost to the lowest total cost. Quality is improved at the source because the mutual confidence and cooperative relationship established between buyer and the single source encourages the vendor to maintain quality products and services.

ASSESSMENT: Rate how well your company is...

4. Ending the practice of awarding business based on price tag alone

The following statements can help to assess the degree to which this one of Dr. Deming's 14 Points is being implemented. Respondents should rank each statement on a five-point scale starting with 0 "not at all true"; 1 "slightly true"; 2 "somewhat true", 3 "mostly true"; and ending with 4, "completely true".

Questions:
1. Supplier selection is based on quality and price rather than price alone.
2. Suppliers are involved in the product/service development process.
3. Long-term relationships are developed with suppliers.
4. There is a reliance on a few dependable suppliers.

Commentary on Chapter 4

Stotz: Every business is a series of activities, or, as Dr. Deming called it, a process. Each activity is connected to the ones prior and the ones after. This is similar to a chain, where each link is connected to the one before and the one after, but also equally connected to all other links in the chain. The result is that you cannot touch any link in the chain without having an impact on all the other links. One of the most frustrating things for my staff and me when I was at Pepsi was when we were given parts and tools that were not the best ones for the job. We could make them work, but it would be a pain to get them working right. It made no sense to us why we would be given these substandard parts or tools. Upon investigation, I was able to find out that the purchasing department had as its goal (as given by its manager) to reduce costs. Someone in the department was probably highly rewarded for the purchase of those substandard parts and tools because of the cost that they saved on the invoice.

But Dr. Deming taught me that business isn't as simple as a low price on an invoice—it's a chain of activities. When you introduce something substandard, or slightly different than the prior components, the system must adjust to the different input. A system with constantly changing inputs will naturally be inefficient because the workers must constantly adjust and calibrate the system to deal with the changes that are brought into it.

In order to reduce the impact of this, Dr. Deming introduced the idea of having only one supplier for the parts and inputs into the system. This was a revolutionary concept at the time, because typically purchasing managers were told to buy from many suppliers. The first perceived benefit of having multiple suppliers was to get the lowest price, as suppliers were pitted against each other. The second perceived benefit was stability in supply, as it was thought that having a few suppliers would mean that if one ran out, then the other would be able to supply.

Dr. Deming changed the focus to developing a long-term relationship with a supplier, not based only on price but on consistency of product and contribution to the improvement of the final product. This was his concept of focusing on total costs. Dr. Deming focused us on the idea that inconsistency in raw materials was causing a lot of trouble down the production line, and that this was a problem that we created ourselves. This reinforced his lesson about getting it right at the beginning of the production process to reduce problems along the chain.

Additional resources

Andrew: http://youtu.be/ue9fHH6CDpM

5 CONSTANTLY IMPROVE THE SYSTEM OF PRODUCTION AND SERVICE

Improve constantly and forever every process for planning, production, and service. Search continually for problems in order to improve every activity in the company, improve quality and productivity, and thus decrease costs. It is management's job to work continually on the system (design, incoming materials, maintenance, improvements of machines, training, supervision, and retraining).

Attack special causes of extreme variation in a process first, then common causes.

To understand "common" and "special" causes of variation in a business process, we must first measure the output of the process on a regular basis. When we start to do this, we usually find that the output bounces around wildly; the system is said to be "out of control." These wildly variable outcomes are usually due to what Deming calls "special causes" of variation; for example, if production equipment is not properly maintained. In the first stage of improving quality, workers and management try to identify and solve these "special causes."

Once solved, Deming refers to the system as being "in control," meaning the output has only random variation occurring tightly around the average; it almost never bounces around. Hence, any variability at that point is only driven by "common causes" of variation. At this stage, worker training to maintain this steady state of production is critical. However, to take the production process to an improved level of output from this point would require more than just training – it would require new thinking, or what Dr. Deming calls "education". From this, we can learn that fixing problems is not improving a process.

First bring the process into control, and then improve the process.

Many people involved with a process mistakenly think that fixing special causes is improving that process, but it is just the first step toward bringing that process under control. Improving a process only happens when a process is in control (special causes have been fixed), resulting in substantially decreased variability of output.

Continuous improvement requires teamwork.

Remember that quality starts with management. If management does not truly believe in the importance of quality, the workers will perceive this and they will not pursue quality. Continuous improvement and reducing defects from the start can only be achieved with teamwork in the initial design stage. Product design staff must be constantly listening to customers and the production staff. Continuous improvement means that the team should be forever continuing to reduce waste and improve processes.

Apply the "Deming Cycle" to continuously improve: Plan, Do, Study, Act.

Improving a system starts with a few questions, such as "What is our objective?" and "What outcome do we predict?" The idea of the "Deming Cycle" came originally from Dr. Deming's mentor, Dr. William Shewart. The idea is rooted in the scientific method, which The Oxford English Dictionary defines as "a method or procedure ... consisting in systematic observation, measurement, and experiment, and the formulation, testing, and modification of hypotheses."

- Plan: Study the current situation. Establish the objectives of the experiment. Predict what outcome should come from the experiment.
- Do: Implement the plan on a trial basis. Collect data. Consider it as if you are doing an experiment.
- Study: Study the actual results and compare these against expected results. Determine if the trial is working correctly. Did the results turn out as predicted? Or not? What can be learned from studying the outcome? Should the theory be modified and another test run?
- Act: Determine where to apply changes and standardize improvements, then apply the improvements and start again. Or, if the results did not turn out as planned, then adjust your plan and prediction and redo the experiment.

Management's new role is to understand statistical thinking and use it to enhance systems.

Management can't intelligently change company systems without understanding statistical thinking. They must provide a setting wherein workers can be successful. Their job is to spot and remove anything that is preventing good work. Finally, they must understand that their focus should be on reducing variation, not blaming events and people, which are almost always exhibiting normal variation.

ASSESSMENT: Rate how well your company is...

5. Constantly improving the system of production and service

The following statements can help to assess the degree to which this one of Dr. Deming's 14 Points is being implemented. Respondents should rank each statement on a five point scale starting with 0 "not at all true"; 1 "slightly true"; 2 "somewhat true", 3 "mostly true"; and ending with 4, "completely true".

Questions:

1. Customers' requirements are analyzed in the process of developing a product/service.

2. Customers' feedback is used to continually improve the product/service.

3. Top management assesses its competitors in order to improve the product/service.

Commentary on Chapter 5

Stotz: Once the management team understands the concept of a system, it's their job to constantly focus on how to improve that system. Rather than focusing on the good and bad performances of individuals, the focus shifts to building a series of activities that work together efficiently to form a healthy system.

When companies start to implement Dr. Deming's principles they find that shifting the focus away from the people and toward the process is rewarding.

A core principle of this concept is that people can only produce as good a product as the system can produce. If the system is poorly designed with inconsistency in input, then there will be inconsistency in output. It would take massive personal effort by any one employee to change this outcome. In my experience as a young manager, I had the energy to try to improve my own area. But, once I came up against other departments it became much more difficult for me to make an impact. Dr. Deming teaches us that the job of management is to bring together the supervisors or the managers of each activity and encourage them to work together to improve the production system.

Dr. Deming talked a lot about tracking the output of a process to see if it was in "control". He had his famous "red bead" demonstration to help teach people about variation. My description of what he was teaching is this:

Imagine 1,000 people standing in a room and we ask them all to flip a coin. Let's say that the object of this activity is to flip heads consecutively, the person who flips the most consecutive heads is the top performer, and the converse of that, the person who flips the most consecutive tails would be the worst performer.

We say, "If you flip heads, go lean up against the wall on the right side of the room, and tails go to the left." After our first flip the room would be split equally with 500 head flippers against the wall on the right and 500 tail flippers on the left.

Then we tell them all to flip again, and ask the 500 who flipped heads that if they flipped tails, return to their seat. And we do the same for the tail flippers. We will end up with roughly 250 people on the right who flipped heads two times in a row, and 250 on the left side who flipped tails two times in a row.

If we repeated this, we would end up with about 125 people on both walls; then if we did it again, we would end up with about 60 people, then about 30, then about 16 and finally about 8 people remaining on both walls. These 16 people would have flipped heads or tails consecutively seven times.

So in this activity, the eight people who flipped heads seven consecutive times were the obvious best performers and the eight who flipped tails seven consecutive times were the worst performers. But, should they be rewarded and punished? Remember, there is less than a one percent chance to flip heads seven consecutive times. So was it skill or just a normal random output coming from a perfectly random activity?

Dr. Deming taught that just a basic understanding of statistics will tell you that, in any activity, there will be a wide range of outputs and, to focus on those outputs, which are most likely coming from randomness, is to waste time punishing or rewarding people for no good reason. So, Dr. Deming taught me that in a production process it is better to bring together the staff to study the variation of the output in that process and work to reduce variation in that process, rather than focusing on the performance of the individuals.

> **Deming:** Schools of business have done their work. They're not teaching transformation. They're teaching use of visible figures, creative accounting, how to maximize the price of the company's stock by keeping up that quarterly dividend.

Video resources

Andrew: http://youtu.be/PAVa77V3LYE
Dr. Deming: http://youtu.be/-qQSLoFHgO4

6 INSTITUTE TRAINING ON THE JOB

Institute modern methods of training on the job for all, including management, to make better use of every employee. New skills are required to keep up with changes in materials, methods, product and service design, machinery, techniques, and service.

Training to constantly improve systems decreases costs.

Training is an integral part of the system – not just an optional part of staff development. Employees are the key asset of every company; management must acknowledge this, and encourage staff to be involved in achieving company goals. Training enables employees to understand their responsibilities in meeting customer needs. You must provide better training for workers in a wider array of skills, and give them more flexibility in their job assignments.

Workers usually learn from other staff members, who may not have been trained properly. This can result in deviation from standard instructions, and cause workers to develop bad habits that will be passed on to new staff. If people are poorly trained, they will work in a similar way, adding variation to processes.

Training is for everyone— and it does not need to be costly or formal.

Training should reach employees and management – both new and old, as some "old" employees were never trained properly. Managers and supervisors often do not understand the processes they are responsible for keeping in statistical control, so they also need training to acquire information about the process and the company.

Top management needs to be highly strategic, and needs to understand the intricacies of operations. Training results in a valuable but intangible future return.

Some of the best training experiences include group-led efforts that serve as team-building exercises, such as creating training manuals, workshops, webinars, vendor demonstrations, and specific discussions on best practices. Training should include the soft skills, experiences, and knowledge of the entire team. Professional development, coaching, and mentoring should be encouraged and acknowledged.

In many companies, training is often given a low priority, and all too frequently people are shown how to do a task they've never previously done only once before being set loose into the workplace – often without rechecking their progress. Follow-up training is critical.

Education and training are not the same.

Training shows how to do something, while education reveals why we do what we do. Training or learning new skills is vital for workers to keep pace with variations in equipment, methods, product layout and design, appliances, techniques and services and to meet the ever-changing demands of customers. Training must also educate employees about the customers' needs.

Managers should view workers as valuable assets, and staff training as an investment that will yield long-term benefits, not just as a one-off cost. If training is viewed in the wrong way, new staff members may arrive to work on their first day, be trained once, and then never be trained again.

Management will often introduce the guidelines, policies, and layouts for a process. But, when one worker teaches another, practices can gradually start to drift away from the original guidelines. Without management retraining over time, worker misconceptions and mistakes can lead to unfavorable outcomes.

When a person has brought his work to a state of statistical control – whether he was trained well or badly – he has completed his learning of that particular job. It is not economical to try to provide further training of the same kind, as continuation of training by the same method will accomplish nothing.

Avoid the common excuses that management teams often use to avoid training:

- "It's for my people, not for me."
- "It's for manufacturing, not for me."
- "Our problems are different here."
- "We rely on our experience."
- "People learn in different ways."

ASSESSMENT: Rate how well your company is...

6. Instituting training on the job

The following statements can help to assess the degree to which this one of Dr. Deming's 14 Points is being implemented. Respondents should rank each statement on a five point scale starting with 0 "not at all true"; 1 "slightly true"; 2 "somewhat true", 3 "mostly true"; and ending with 4, "completely true".

Questions:

1. Employees are trained in statistical improvement techniques.

2. Employees are trained in quality related matters.

3. Employees are trained in specific work related skills

4. Supervisors are trained in statistical improvement techniques.

Commentary on Chapter 6

Stotz: Training is critical to reach and maintain a level of consistency in a production process. When a management team devotes the time to properly training new staff before they put them into the production process, they are demonstrating to all employees the importance of consistency in the process.

Dr. Deming makes a clear distinction between training and education. Training is focused on making sure that the people involved in any activity within the process are taught the correct way that things should be done. Just throwing someone into a job without adequate training demonstrates to the employee that consistency in that activity is not a high priority.

So training helps set a minimum level of knowledge, skill and consistency. Improvements in any activity can come from consistent training, and these improvements can reduce costs related to that activity. To Dr. Deming, education is less focused on a particular activity. Rather, it is much more broad, almost to be considered as exploring the world around you, searching for new knowledge. And, Dr. Deming taught that opening up minds to explore new things and new ways is what education is all about, and [that] is how new ideas can come into a company.

Deming: When you think of all the underuse, abuse, and misuse of the people of this country, this may be the world's most underdeveloped nation. Number one, we did it again! We're number one, for underdevelopment.

Our people not used, mismanaged, misused, abused, and underused, by a management that worships sacred cows, a style of management that was never right but made good fortune for this country between 1950 and 1968 because the rest of the world, so much of it, was devastated. You couldn't go wrong no matter what you did.

Video resources

Andrew: http://youtu.be/xdrB8lUKexg

Dr. Deming: http://youtu.be/lBZdxcig-wE

7 INSTITUTE LEADERSHIP

Adopt and institute leadership aimed at helping people do a better job. The responsibility of managers and supervisors must become quality, not quantity. Improvement of quality will automatically improve productivity. Management must ensure that immediate action is taken to fix inherited defects, poor maintenance requirements, poor tools, fuzzy operational definitions, and all conditions detrimental to quality.

Take immediate action when workers inform.

The responsibility of managers and supervisors must be changed from just focusing on production or financial numbers to focusing on quality. Improvement of quality will automatically improve productivity. Management must ensure that immediate action is taken on reports of defects, maintenance requirements, poor tools, unclear operational definitions, and other obstacles to quality.

Leadership inspires people to work together toward a common goal.

Leaders are essential elements of any company. They are efficient, systematic, skillful, hardworking, and practical. They get support from enough people in power to make things happen. They have ideas and are realistic about realizing them. Leadership is more about having the ability to lead people than it is about managing. It means guiding and coaching people rather than ruling them. Supervisors serve as a vital link between managers and workers. They first need training in quality management before they can work as role models and leaders, and before they can effectively communicate management's commitment to improving quality.

Remember, instituting leadership is management's job, not a supervisor's job. Eliminate the focus on outcome (hitting targets and "managing by objective"). Leaders must understand the work they oversee.

Managers control— leaders support and coach.

Managers emphasize the rules, standards and specifications. They try to stop people from doing things the wrong way, and they strive for zero defects. Managers act like police, monitoring and enforcing performance. Leaders coach people instead of commanding them. They try to assist people in living up to their full potential. Leaders try to remove barriers to pride of workmanship. Leaders develop people in all respects. Leaders understand the work they supervise. Most importantly, leaders know the difference between "special" and "common" cause variations.

A leader encourages, motivates, and supports employees in their efforts to bring the company to life.

Most problems that exist in companies are not due to absence of management, but to absence of leadership. A leader converts the company's aims into actions that awaken and encourage workers. People working with this inspired mindset inevitably accomplish something unique for the customer.

Old-school supervisors ask people to be silent about problems for the good of the team. They solve conflict through pressure or compromise. Leaders bring conflicts out into the open so that differences can be sorted out and "win-win" solutions can be found, instead of "win-lose" hierarchical decisions.

Leaders understand statistical thinking and focus on improving the system.

Leaders direct an organization through the stages of transformation. Leaders recognize the difference between special and common causes of variation in production. Managers force people to work harder even though the source of faults is not worker performance, but the system in which workers are stuck.

It is a leader's duty to remove system-caused problems by allowing people to study and improve the underlying system, not by blaming employees for situations beyond their control. If a leader wants the company to succeed, she must help the employees succeed. Here are some quotes on the subject from Dr. Deming:

- "A leader's job is to help people and to know when people need special help."
- "If a worker cannot learn his job, why did you put him there?"
- "I used to say that people are assets, not commodities. But they are not just assets: They are jewels."
- "Why lead? People happier, quality up, productivity up, everybody wins."

ASSESSMENT: Rate how well your company is...

7. Instituting leadership

The following statements can help to assess the degree to which this one of Dr. Deming's 14 Points is being implemented. Respondents should rank each statement on a five point scale starting with 0 "not at all true"; 1 "slightly true"; 2 "somewhat true", 3 "mostly true"; and ending with 4, "completely true".

Questions:

1. Supervisors help their employees on the job.
2. Supervisors work to build the trust of their employees.
3. Supervisors lead in a way that is consistent with the aims of the organization.
4. Supervisors are viewed as coaches by their employees.

Commentary on Chapter 7

Stotz: Looking back at my first class with Dr. Deming, I can clearly recall his level of frustration with the state of management of companies (as he saw it). He didn't feel that there was much management or leadership going on in companies, and he felt that the workers were being abandoned and just told what to do. As he saw it, management felt that their job was done by issuing the orders and going back to their offices. What Dr. Deming taught was that leaders at the top of an organization oversee managers, who oversee workers. Once leadership is improved—and this was the first task for any company trying to transform itself—the next focus was on the managers who oversaw the workers. Once this was addressed, then the focus shifted to helping the workers regain pride of workmanship.

During a Q&A session in my first seminar with Dr Deming, I recall an audience member mentioning that "You are the father of the TQM [total quality management] movement." Dr. Deming interrupted the guy and asked, "What is TQM?" This shocked the audience. Dr. Deming then went on to explain that TQM was a label assigned by people, but that what he was talking about was transforming management and reducing the variation in a process.

> **Deming:** Point Number Seven is improvement of leadership, which we commonly call "supervision". I think that it should be called "leadership", leading people to help them to do a better job, be it in management or on the factory floor. Supervision should be replaced by leadership.
>
> And there's no secret, once again, about what leadership is, what leadership must do. It's to help people.

Video resources

Andrew: http://youtu.be/Dspnv4FJNBw
Dr. Deming: http://youtu.be/bazaVOEax-A

8 DRIVE OUT FEAR IN THE WORKPLACE

Encourage effective two-way communication and drive out fear throughout the organization so that everybody may work effectively and more productively for the company.

Fear is the enemy of creativity and progress.

Fear suppresses two of quality's foundations, innovation and continual improvement. A fearful team can never produce fresh concepts. Instead, that team will cover up its mistakes and learn nothing about the improvement of processes. Fear is the inner voice that prevents us from expressing or communicating ideas. It increases employee turnover and causes breakdowns in quality. Fear is the opposite of joy in work.

Be subtle, helpful, and positive amid worker errors.

When mistakes occur, strong criticism will only slow down motivation and expansion. Instead, be subtle, with constructive criticism and the goal of helping the worker succeed. Tell the worker that you believe he can solve the problem, and let him know that he is valued. Fear is the root of a great amount of waste and loss. Fearful workers take whatever action possible to get rid of the cause of the fear, which is never in the company's best interest. Fear deprives people of pride in their work and kills motivation. It makes people defensive, stopping them from sharing with management what's really happening on the factory floor. Without an atmosphere of mutual respect, no statistically based system of management can work— nor any other system.

Look for symptoms of fear in the workplace:
- Fear of job loss or negative impact on reviews.
- Fear of being teased by managers or peers.
- Fear of being blamed for a dispute.
- Fear of disappointing managers.
- Fear of appearing silly due to making an error.
- Fear of missing a deadline or causing someone else to lose face.

Fear of change is a big barrier to overcome. Remember, people don't resist change – they resist being changed! The goal is for everyone to be part of the change and to own the change process.

Understand the underlying causes of fear in the workplace:
- Absence of stable processes, systems, or environments.
- Lack of real guidance or training.
- A lack of the means necessary to perform the work (for example: equipment, time, or personnel).
- Absence of faith and trust between team members and in the project's leadership.
- Conflicting objectives in the organization.
- Inept, unqualified managers or supervisors who fear empowering their employees.

Act to remove fear in the workplace.
Management must create an environment that staff can

be proud of, where staff can find happiness in their work. Instead of accusing the workers, management must fix the system for them. Continuous improvement requires good data. If workers are afraid of the consequences of data, they won't report data accurately.

Guide employees when they need it. If they aren't confident in their ability to do the job, don't expect their best performance. Empower your employees. This means providing them with the materials, information, and support necessary to carry out their tasks.

Always be open to listening to the views of all employees. Help workers to feel that they are part of a team, and that they have input into how the business operates. Work to make sure that employees' ideas don't get trapped somewhere on a manager's desk. If management encourages two-way communication and builds trust, team members will be more interested in disclosing their suggestions, and in challenging established processes. This point is one of the most important for management to work on, because it affects the outcome of many of Deming's 14 Points, including those on breaking down departmental barriers, ceasing dependence on mass inspection, education and training, stopping slogans, ceasing to award business to suppliers based on price alone, eliminating standards, and facilitating continuous improvement.

ASSESSMENT: Rate how well your company is...

8. Driving out fear

The following statements can help to assess the degree to which this one of Dr. Deming's 14 Points is being implemented. Respondents should rank each statement on a five point scale starting with 0 "not at all true"; 1 "slightly true"; 2 "somewhat true", 3 "mostly true"; and ending with 4, "completely true".

Questions:

1. Employees express new ideas related to improving work conditions.

2. Employees seek their supervisors' assistance when unsure of their tasks.

3. Employees are not afraid to report working conditions that interfere with quality.

4. Employees feel they have job security.

Commentary on Chapter 8

Stotz: One of the problems that Dr. Deming saw as he traveled around the world looking at businesses was that management focused on the output of the process. So, rather than involving employees in the design, development and improvement of the production process, the worker was stripped of that involvement and told only to get to work and hit targets. When I sat and listened to Dr. Deming speak in his seminars, I started thinking that he was an idealistic dreamer—and my further understanding of his teaching ended up supporting this! Dr. Deming thought that the best way to build a great business was to create a company where workers wanted to come to work, where they weren't intimidated or simply not listened to.

He taught that once managers start to understand that there is natural variation in any process, they start shifting their focus from punishing those workers who ended up on the bottom and rewarding those workers who ended up on the top.

These managers start to understand that most of the outcome of the process is random and not necessarily under the control of the worker. With this understanding, managers shift their thinking to the whole system or the production process, not to the worker. When this happens, the worker is invited to join in improving the system. This worker involvement starts to drive fear out of the workplace.

Video resources

Andrew: http://youtu.be/PrUjmULKeu0

9 BREAK DOWN BARRIERS BETWEEN DEPARTMENTS

People in research, design, sales, and production must work as a team in order to foresee problems of production and usage that may affect the product or service.

Barriers between departments block a common vision.

A company's different departments rarely have overall goals that clash, but departments rarely function as one team, so they can't see or resolve the larger issues of the organization. Even worse, one unit's goal may cause difficulty for another. The mistaken belief that one department is more important than another is often detrimental to projects and the organization as a whole.

Innovation and endless improvement come as departments in a business work more closely together. This cannot be done when departments are behind barriers. Barriers remain when departments have different aims and fail to work together to solve problems, specify policies, or assign new tasks. Misaligned departmental goals lead to an ineffective organization, while common goals bring unity and strength.

Barriers cause sub-optimization and unexceptional company outcomes.

Barriers breed sub-optimization—i.e., they force processes, procedures, and systems to give less than the best possible outcome. Barriers are mostly caused by lack of coordination and communication between different departments. One of the most crucial differences between old and new-style management is how shop-floor employees, supervisors, department heads, middle managers, and senior managers view their jobs— Is their job to work only for their department and its boss (which usually leads to sub-optimization), or is it to work for the company? It can't be both. It is up to senior management to ensure that individuals or departments are not blindly pursuing what is best only for them, without considering the impact on the rest of the organization.

One clear example of sub-optimization is an increase in paperwork, resulting in considerable inefficiency, frustration, and cost. It is often the case that the department demanding the paperwork never stops to consider the burden this puts on the rest of the organization.

Leadership promotes unity among departments.

Deming once said, "Teamwork is the ability to work together toward a common vision." For organizational effectiveness, all parts of a company should work as a whole toward company goals for customer satisfaction – not toward individual or departmental goals. If each department boss thinks or is told that her objective is to maximize her unit's profits, the company will fail.

Instead of restricting access to information about their work, all departments must work in harmony and not be divided by departmental possessiveness. A divided company will struggle to achieve its targets. Harmony helps the workforce overcome disputes and develop exceptional products and services. It's not a modern technique that is needed, but rather channels for communicating with employees, and ways of ranking priorities.

Managers must push departments to share information.

Management must smash the barriers that suppress the sharing of information between organizational units. It is also management's duty to promote teamwork, encourage staff to work together on projects, and stop thinking departmentally. Employees must be inspired to think about what is best for the organization. Deming said, "Teamwork creates an unexpected result called 'synergy' in which the whole becomes greater than the sum of the individuals." Employees should learn to see their internal departments as customers and suppliers to other departments in the organization.

Use staff rotations to break down barriers.

Once managers have built an environment of cooperation among departments, they can break through barriers by temporarily moving employees to other departments and exposing them to situations outside of their comfort zones. This might cause a short-term productivity loss while workers are away from their specialty area, but it will create long-term growth for the project and the company. This approach benefits the company by building a larger pool of "generalists", that is, employees skilled in many subjects. New experiences are strong motivators; they broaden a person's view and open them up to more innovative ideas. It is important to note that if management has not yet removed departmental incentives and rewards, rotating staff through those departments does nothing except frustrate the staff being rotated. It is also important to break down physical barriers between staff areas, such as partitions or departments separated on different floors of an office building.

ASSESSMENT: Rate how well your company is...

9. Breaking down barriers among departments

The following statements can help to assess the degree to which this one of Dr. Deming's 14 Points is being implemented. Respondents should rank each statement on a five point scale starting with 0 "not at all true"; 1 "slightly true"; 2 "somewhat true", 3 "mostly true"; and ending with 4, "completely true".

Questions:

1. Different departments have compatible goals.
2. In the product/service design process, there is teamwork among departments.
3. There is good communication among departments.

Commentary on Chapter 9

Stotz: Build a common vision—this is most critical. For business to happen successfully, a long chain of events needs to occur in the right order and in the right way. Yet in many of the steps, the objectives of the different departments or workgroups are opposing. Suppliers want to get the highest price, but customers want the lowest price. The purchasing department wants to get the lowest price for a part, but manufacturing wants to get the right part so that production won't break down. Salespeople always want the product available for delivery to their customers now, while managers want to maintain as little inventory on hand as possible.

To be successful, management must make sure that each department (or person) understands that if each group pursues its own self-interest, it may optimize that department's output, but it may also cause sub-optimization of the output of the overall company. This sub-optimization can range from mild to almost wholly dysfunctional. It is the job of managers and leaders of a company to prevent people from only focusing on their own areas. Instead, they need to be shown the whole chain of events and required to work with other departments.

At CoffeeWORKS, we have a weekly meeting between all department heads. The purpose of the meeting is to build teamwork, and to build understanding of the demands being put on each department. In addition, our objective is to make sure that the management team feels like one cohesive whole. From this, we want to make sure that the workers in the company see the management team acting as a whole, rather than allowing it to become broken up into factions (because factions lead to sub-optimization). The concept of optimizing a system is similar to the workings of an orchestra—of course any one player could play to the extremes of his ability, but this would lead to sub-optimization, as the whole sound of the orchestra would become erratic.

Additional resources:
Andrew: http://youtu.be/YYnSqFFG7Cs

10 ELIMINATE SLOGANS, CHEERLEADING, AND TARGETS

Eliminate slogans, exhortations, and targets for the workforce that ask for zero defects and new levels of productivity. Such exhortations only create adversarial relationships, as the bulk of the causes of low quality and low productivity belong to the system, and thus lie beyond the power of the workforce.

Get rid of posters with slogans, catchphrases, and targets.

Remove posters that state slogans such as "Your work is your self-portrait", "Zero Defects!", "Safety is Your Responsibility!", "Do it Right the First Time!", or "Our goal is to please the customer at all times!" Such slogans insult workers' intelligence. They're directed at the wrong group, and they generate frustration and resentment. Managers often feel such mottos transfer their responsibility to the employees, but there is simply no replacement for leadership. Defect elimination, a safe workplace, and customer satisfaction all start with senior management. It is their task to improve the system for employees, not the other way around.

Slogans wrongly claim that the problem is with the worker, not the system.

A common myth persists within top management, that motivational phrases and posters encourage employees. In fact, they usually have the opposite effect, and the actual result is that management wastes time and money putting them up on the wall. The main drawback of slogans is that they address a specific issue and provide a specific action for employees to follow. They miss the point that the majority of a worker's output is a product of the system.

These catchphrases have never inspired anyone to do a high-quality job. Running to meet targets often shifts employees' focus from long-term customer satisfaction to the short term. Take the phrase: "Do It Right the First Time." It teaches nothing, but places pressure on the worker, because any responsibility is taken away from management and supervisors and placed on the worker. Yet errors are usually due to a lack of training, knowledge, or experience – all of which are management's responsibility. It is the manager's job to train and recruit the right people and put them in the right jobs. Avoid simply telling others to do better without helping them to do so.

Use posters to show what you are doing to improve the work environment and quality.

"Posters that explain to everyone on the job what the management is doing month by month to (for example) purchase better quality of incoming materials from fewer suppliers, better maintenance, or to provide better training, or statistical aids and better supervision to improve quality and productivity, not by working harder but by working smarter, would be a totally different story: They would boost morale. People would then understand that the management is taking some responsibility for hang-ups and defects, and is trying to remove obstacles." -Dr. Deming

Remove numerical targets.

This doesn't mean we completely get rid of numbers — we do need goals to achieve, directions in which to progress, aims to fulfill, and objectives to complete. But we must skip erratic numerical goals.

Yes, budgets and estimates are vital for planning and resource allocation, but still, there must be no random numerical targets. For instance, a salesperson's task is basically to sell as much as she can. With eyes on that target, she may sell a customer a more costly machine than the customer wants, or promise to arrange a shipment instantly, causing delays for other customers. Neither of those clients is likely to become repeat customers. Instead, they may become dedicated enemies of the company! Using this strategy, customers and the company suffer.

Knowledge, training, guidance, systems, techniques, and methods are also required to make it feasible for goals and objectives to be fulfilled. When numerical targets are not achieved, management must study the system rather than blaming the workers.

ASSESSMENT: Rate how well your company is...

10. Eliminating slogans and targets

The following statements can help to assess the degree to which this one of Dr. Deming's 14 Points is being implemented. Respondents should rank each statement on a five point scale starting with 0 "not at all true"; 1 "slightly true"; 2 "somewhat true", 3 "mostly true"; and ending with 4, "completely true".

Questions:

1. Top management provides its workers with the methods/procedures to meet goals.

2. Top management, not the hourly workers, is responsible for removing obstacles that cause defects/errors.

3. Top management does not use vague slogans (i.e. "Do It Right the First Time") in communicating with its employees.

Commentary on Chapter 10

Stotz: Ralph Waldo Emerson once said, "Your actions speak so loudly I cannot hear what you are saying." A quality-focused business that follows Deming's 14 points does not need to shout at its workers and put up posters and slogans. Workers can feel that quality is most important to their bosses. They understand that providing the right product and service to the right customer at the right time and at the right price is the main objective. These workers know that they could stop the whole production process if they saw something going wrong. They understand that they could complain to the purchasing department if they find them just trying to buy the cheapest parts—an action that would negatively impact the system and the output.

A sign on the wall is the work of a lazy manager, and it backfires, because workers are being told one thing, but they know that, when it comes to crunch time, the boss doesn't truly believe it. As Dr. Deming saw it, the fatal flaw of slogans and targets was that it made people believe that the variation among workers was the cause of the problem, instead of just the normal variation of the system. This misdirection of management attention was felt by the workers, and they felt blamed. They didn't understand why other workers would be rewarded—and then later punished—when they could all see that there was only so much that the workers could do with what was provided for them.

Additional resources:
   Andrew: http://youtu.be/SHi6CnK13P0

11 ELIMINATE NUMERICAL QUOTAS FOR THE WORKFORCE AND NUMERICAL GOALS FOR MANAGEMENT

Eliminate work standards (quotas) on the factory floor. Eliminate management by objective and management by numbers and numerical goals. Instead, substitute with leadership.

Quotas and benchmarks make quantity – not quality – the priority.

Quotas and benchmarks can sometimes cause unintended consequences. For instance, they often cause huge costs to be incurred. Fear of job loss can compel employees to meet quotas at any price, without worrying about harming the company. Quotas and benchmarks are usually a guarantee of inefficiency and high costs.

Production targets encourage delivery of poor-quality goods. Work standards and numerical goals are the main creators of fear. Quotas are a short-term solution; they produce results by sacrificing processes. The main effect of numerical quotas on the whole system is to impede quality.

In fact, quotas can reduce production rates, because the priority becomes meeting quotas, rather than driving the company forward.

Set goals as a team, with clear ways to achieve them.

Numerical standards and goals set by management – especially if they are not accompanied by achievable courses of action – have a negative effect. Instead, set goals in a teamwork fashion – management, supervisors and workers – along with methods to achieve them. All employees should learn the use and capabilities of processes, and how to make them better.

Monitor the system and its processes that produce good results. If the system is "in control" – with only predictable and acceptable variation – it can be continually improved to increase productivity. If the system is "out of control," there's no point in setting a goal. Only disappointment and low confidence will result.

Management must put the systems into place to achieve quality results.

It is management's duty to be sure that processes and systems are in place to produce the most favorable outcomes in quality and quantity. If an employee has to do 20 surveys a night, she may finish all 20 early and then have time to waste, or even do harm. At another time, she may fail to complete her surveys. So how will she meet the quota? It's simple. She will take wrongful shortcuts to complete the assignment. For instance, she might use results from other teammates or fake the survey. In any case, finishing sooner or not at all ruins quality and efficiency.

Improve the system, rather than setting individual or team goals.

Setting goals and targets in response to an issue, without first understanding and addressing the root causes in the processes, will only lead to numerous quality issues. A company can remove quotas and work standards, as well as guarantee that workers won't waste time, if it discards fear, upgrades systems, and builds an environment in which workers are fond of their work. Remember, employees are a company treasure.

Ultimately, a company needs to shift from Management by Objectives (MBO) to Management by Planning. MBO tends to weaken long-term results rather than improve them. Objectives are typically set in negotiations between supervisor and employee, thus creating no place for innovation or improvement in processes.

Management by planning emphasizes process, not outcome.

Companies and individuals need goals, intentions, and aims – but not in isolation. They need the education, training, systems, and methods to attain these goals. What they don't need is arbitrary numerical goals— though, of course, a company still needs budgets and forecasts for the planning and allocation of resources.

ASSESSMENT: Rate how well your company is...

11. Eliminating numerical quotas
The following statements can help to assess the degree to which this one of Dr. Deming's 14 Points is being implemented. Respondents should rank each statement on a five point scale starting with 0 "not at all true"; 1 "slightly true"; 2 "somewhat true", 3 "mostly true"; and ending with 4, "completely true".

Questions:
1. Work standards are based on quality and quantity rather than quantity alone.
2. Work standards are set based on process capability studies.
3. Numerical quotas are not given higher priority than quality of workmanship.

Commentary on Chapter 11

Stotz: I was a recent university graduate in the area of finance when I got my first job as a supervisor at Pepsi in Los Angeles. It was during this time that I asked my boss if I could attend a Deming seminar. That was 1989, and management by objectives was a very popular topic in the area of leadership. MBO, as it was called, made sense to me: Sit down with the manager or employee and mutually decide upon the objectives, then provide the resources and get out of the way so that they could achieve the objectives. When I first heard Dr. Deming say to stop using management by objectives and management by numbers, I didn't know what to make of it.

What I learned was that we should stop focusing on the wrong things, like the volume of output or getting work done. I learned that we should shift our focus to quality, and our attention to the customer's needs. Dr. Deming taught that you can only truly make this happen by addressing the whole system of the business; by getting everybody focused on quality; by shifting the focus from objectives (or outputs) to planning and preparing (with a new focus on inputs and process).

Rather than setting individual goals between an employee and their direct boss (which often leads to sub-optimization), we need to be focused on team goals. At first I thought that Dr. Deming was advocating a system with no goals or objectives. But I later learned, that was not the case. To prevent sub-optimization, it was important to set goals, but to have those goals focused on the inputs and to balance those goals between departments.

Additional resources
    Andrew: http://youtu.be/RYdCTXzIP4Y

12 REMOVE BARRIERS TO PRIDE OF WORKMANSHIP

Remove barriers that rob management, engineers, and hourly workers of their right to pride of workmanship. To do this, abolish annual merit rating and management by objectives. Give people dignity in their work, and they will provide a higher quality product.

If management does not care about workers, it becomes hard to find good ones.

It's difficult enough to find skilled workers. It is harder still to find qualified people who believe in providing an efficient day's work for an honest day's pay and want to develop with and help the business prosper. Signs of the problem: Lack of interest in the job, and the feeling that goals, targets, or expectations can't be achieved. Roots of the problem: A company has ever-changing goals and can't settle on any one goal for very long, management doesn't care about workers' problems, poor training in technological developments, no communication between employees and management, insufficient documentation on how to do the task, absence of materials, training, and staff to correctly perform tasks. Merit ratings mostly result in negative outcomes – workers get blamed by management for failing to meet targets, when the real weakness lies with management.

Make work a pleasant place where people can enjoy pride in workmanship.

Make work a more pleasant place to be by preventing disputes. Offer worker outings such as picnics, field trips, sporting events, and work-based game events. This can result in a team-friendly workforce.

Create systems that let people take pride in their work. This boosts confidence. Give clear goals and objectives – many organizations fail to give sufficient direction and measurable objectives. Remove appraisal systems— such rankings delight the boss, not the customer, and create conflict, competition, and embarrassment. These systems only serve to destroy a worker's natural motivation and happiness with their work.

Provide resources to perform tasks. One common mistake is to assign a task, job, or goal, and fail to allot enough time to finish it. Managers must accurately plan how long a task should take, and ensure that workers have the tools to do the job properly. Machinery that breaks down is the fault of management negligence and has a negative effect on morale.

Pride of workmanship is the worker's birthright.

People enjoy the feeling of helping others, which contradicts the common misconception that people only value money, holidays, and power. The satisfaction gained from helping people is unique.

Everyone should feel that their work is recognized, valuable, and essential to the company's success. Supervisors should ask workers: "What keeps you from being able to do a good job?" and then act on the answers. People are usually keen to do well, and become disheartened when they can't.

Too often, misguided supervision, faulty equipment,

and defective materials stand in the way of good performance. Eliminate such hurdles.

Education adds to quality and improves self-esteem.

Institute a vigorous education program and urge self-improvement for everyone. A company needs good people, but it also needs people who are constantly improving. A company's or an individual's advances in competitive position are rooted in knowledge. Dr. Deming said, "We're not here to learn skills; we're here for education – to learn theory." Training for a skill is limited – it ends when ability has reached a reliable state. In comparison, education is never-ending.

The future is important, and education is vital for improving the future.

One barrier to success is thinking that you have successfully "installed quality control". This thinking is a mistake, because the job of improving quality is never finished.

Broaden education to help broaden employees' development.

A company should take action to aid and encourage the education of its employees at all levels. Courses should no longer be restricted to training, but should be broadened to include good educational content. Companies should also compile lists of courses available locally – as well as prerequisites and other information – and encourage employees to take advantage of these courses.

ASSESSMENT: Rate how well your company is...

12. Removing barriers to pride in workmanship

The following statements can help to assess the degree to which this one of Dr. Deming's 14 Points is being implemented. Respondents should rank each statement on a five point scale starting with 0 "not at all true"; 1 "slightly true"; 2 "somewhat true", 3 "mostly true"; and ending with 4, "completely true".

Questions:

1. Performance appraisals are not used to rank employees.
2. The quality of the working environment is good.
3. There is adequate documentation on how to do the job.
4 There is no pressure for short-term results.
5. Top management sets realistic goals for its employees.

Commentary on Chapter 12

Stotz: In his seminar, Dr. Deming shocked us all as he told us to throw out management by objectives, and throw out annual ratings or reviews. Most of us in the audience had never heard anything like that. In fact, we were trained on these methods, and they made sense to us. But Dr. Deming's point was to stop focusing on the wrong things—that we would never move to a higher level of quality and satisfaction in the workforce until we started focusing on the right things. What were the right things? To create a workplace where people felt cared about and listened to, and where they felt pride in what they did. Bring pride of workmanship back to the employee. Bring in training and education, and make it available to all workers. Help workers to reach for their next level of development.

Detaching from the old ways of thinking is particularly hard to do—even at CoffeeWORKS, we still do performance reviews. We try to keep them short and simple, and more of a feedback and discussion opportunity, but we still do them. I have found this to be one of the biggest challenges for me in Dr. Deming's philosophy.

Deming: The annual system of rating salaried people, known also as merit system, annual appraisal of performance, annual rating of performance, known also under the name "management by objective". Someone in Germany called it "management by fear", which is still better.

Pay for merit, pay for what you get, reward performance, sounds great. It can't be done.

Unfortunately, it cannot be done on short range. After 10 years, perhaps, 20 years, yes. But Americans have, somehow become obsessed, from many years back and nobody knows where it originated, that everybody must be appraised.

Now, the effect is devastating. People have to have something to show, something to count. In other words, the system, merit system nourishes short-term performance and annihilates long-term planning. It annihilates teamwork. People cannot work together. To get a promotion, you have to get ahead. By working with a team, you help other people. You may help yourself equally, but you don't get ahead. By being equal, you get ahead by being ahead, produce something more, have more to show, more to count.

Teamwork means – work together, hear everybody's ideas, fill in for other people's weaknesses, acknowledge their strengths, and work together.

It's impossible under the merit rating and review of performance. People are afraid. They're in fear. They work in fear. They cannot contribute to the company as they would wish to contribute.

Video resources:
  Andrew: http://youtu.be/n46irQUxzN4
  Dr. Deming: http://youtu.be/Oi6bC4obHxo

13 INSTALL A STRONG PROGRAM OF EDUCATION AND SELF-IMPROVEMENT

Institute a vigorous program of education, and encourage self-improvement for everyone. Everybody must learn to grow.

Managers play a vital part in workforce education.

Inspire self-education, produce a company training catalogue, and honor knowledge and professionalism. These are the ingredients necessary for lasting employment and long-term business success.

Top executives must reject the idea that spending on education is a misuse of money and time. Just as we reinvest in other resources, we must reinvest in an organization's most important treasure – its people. Management must make clear from the beginning their devotion to this concept and must spend time and effort to establish the continuous improvement philosophy in the system.

Gains made through learning are priceless.

It is crazy to believe that the gains of what is spent on

education can be measured. Education is precious, beyond estimation. It is significant for improving the future and it is where quality control starts and ends.

Education and retraining is about investing in people, which is a prerequisite for long-term planning. People must take hold of extra knowledge and skills. Education and training will assist people in fitting into their new jobs and roles. Training should not be viewed as just an expense, or something that goes away, but rather as an investment that can last a lifetime.

Promote general education and knowledge gain.

Encourage staff to regularly upgrade their knowledge of quality and testing techniques through seminars and classes. Provide bonuses to the team for attending new seminars and starting special interest groups. Retrain individuals to refresh their skills in quality management. Managers should encourage all employees to pursue general education rather than just training through the company's own courses.

Training is for all employees at all levels of the company.

Training must be provided for all levels within the company – workers, supervisors, new recruits, and managers alike. Knowledge must not be judged on the basis of employees' time with the company. Rather, everyone in the organization must receive education. Self-improvement should not be limited to obvious areas of operations. Instead, people should be encouraged to pick whatever activities they think will help them grow. Management and employees should be up-to-date in new knowledge and procedures.

Recruit skilled people who show evidence of a strong desire to continue education.

When hiring new staff, demand not just skilled people, but people who are progressing with education. Those rising to leadership positions will still have their roots in knowledge. Scan for people who are learning and interested in learning, who are improving and eager to improve, rather than spending time focusing on former new recruits.

Of course, an organization needs to train its people, but management must also realize that traditional job training can sometimes lead to passing on mistakes and inefficiencies of the past. Therefore, it is education that often drives a company to a new level of performance.

Lastly, remember that almost all substantial advances in thinking come from things that people said were too theoretical or impractical. So, encourage abstract thinking and education to help open the minds of all employees.

ASSESSMENT: Rate how well your company is...

13. Instituting education and self-improvement

The following statements can help to assess the degree to which this one of Dr. Deming's 14 Points is being implemented. Respondents should rank each statement on a five point scale starting with 0 "not at all true"; 1 "slightly true"; 2 "somewhat true", 3 "mostly true"; and ending with 4, "completely true".

Questions:
1. There are programs to develop teamwork among employees.
2. There are programs to develop effective communication among employees.
3. There are programs to develop employees' conflict resolution skills.
4. There are programs to broaden employees' skills for future organizational needs.

Commentary on Chapter 13

Stotz: Dr. Deming makes a strong distinction between education and training. Training is focused on maintaining the consistency of the output of a particular activity. It is valuable for bringing on new employees in the right way, so as not to allow an activity to drift and lose its consistency of output. At times, training can bring new ideas and allow workers to discuss and test new ways of doing things; but Dr. Deming was pretty clear that training could never achieve what could be achieved by education.

Dr. Deming pushed us all to go back to our jobs and focus on [the] general education of the workforce. I can recall him saying, "Without theory there is no learning." We had to have a starting point and then study, test and learn to gain new knowledge. His idea was to open up education opportunities to all employees in the company, allowing employees to pursue a wide array of learning. As employees felt the challenge of learning new things, they would bring these new things back to the operations of the business and improve it. In addition, they would be learning about the process of learning—learning to ask questions, and then to investigate and answer those questions and improve the operations based upon what they [had] learned. Dr. Deming's concept of plan, do, check and act was a great example of the process of learning.

Deming: Point 13 is self-improvement; a program of self-improvement, education, improvement in other ways, helping people to live better, education in whatever one's fancy might take him into – history, music, archeology, anything whatever to keep people's minds developing.
Education need not be connected with work. Maybe better if it's not. Point Number 6 is training and retraining for the job. Point Number 13 is elevating people's minds. No organization can survive with just good people. They need people that are improving.

Video resources:
Andrew: http://youtu.be/4aH-Xddrtac
Dr. Deming: http://youtu.be/GSdBeSrNiXU

14 GET EVERYONE INVOLVED IN ACHIEVING THE TRANSFORMATION

Put everybody in the company to work to accomplish the transformation. The transformation is everybody's job.

Top management needs to inspire action on all the 14 points.

To carry out the entire quality mission, a top management team with a plan of action is needed. The whole workforce must be engaged in the change. No employee, supervisor or manager can achieve it alone.

If carrying out the entire quality mission is the job of top management, the task of producing quality products or services is everyone's task – not only experts in the quality control unit, not just top management, and certainly not just workers.

All workers, including managers, must have a precise idea of how to "progressively enhance quality". Ultimately though, the effort must come from top management, which has the most control and influence. They are the leaders. To accomplish this, first make sure that every assignment and task is part of a process.

As soon as the resolution is made at the top, bring

middle management, supervisors, and employees on board. This requires training and eradication of inhibitions (fear, competition, worry, boundaries, and divisions). Everyone must support each other fully to consistently improve the system. Think methodically.

Chart the change of each company system with input from all staff.

Use a flow chart to divide a process into stages. Then ask questions about what changes should be made at each stage to improve the efficiency of other upstream or downstream stages. Involve everyone in improving the input and output of the stages. Give all members of all teams a chance to add ideas and principles, but always keep teams focused on the ultimate objective of meeting the wants and needs of the consumer.

Management's worldview must adjust to changes in order to succeed.

To succeed in transformational accomplishments, management must see things in a fresh way. Never indulge in the rat-race business of increasing quarterly profits. Be in the profession of satisfying customers and workers. Automatically, profits will most likely rise.

Management transforms the company by helping all employees internalize the 14 points.

Fight to make sure all staff members internalize the 14 points. Take pleasure in the new philosophy. Include all of the company's employees. Everyone is vital to the change. Study and apply Dr. Deming's "Plan, Do, Study, Act" cycle.

Top management must stay on the front line of change.

Clearly define top management's permanent commitment to ever-improving quality and productivity, and their obligations to apply all of these principles. Indeed, it is not enough that top management commit themselves for life to quality and productivity. They must know what it is that they are committed to – that is, what they must do.

Create a structure in top management that will push the preceding 13 points every day, and take action to accomplish the transformation. Support is not enough: action is required. Learn and adopt the new philosophy, and put everyone to work on it and in it.

ASSESSMENT: Rate how well your company is...

14. Taking action to accomplish the transformation

The following statements can help to assess the degree to which this one of Dr. Deming's 14 Points is being implemented. Respondents should rank each statement on a five point scale starting with 0 "not at all true"; 1 "slightly true"; 2 "somewhat true", 3 "mostly true"; and ending with 4, "completely true".

Questions:

1. Top management takes action toward executing its quality improvement policies.
2. Top management makes its quality improvement policies visible to all employees.
3. Top management relies on internal and external consultants to implement its quality improvement policies.

Commentary on Chapter 14

Stotz: Once senior management has made a full commitment to Deming's 14 points—and has trained the next level of managers, and these managers have trained workers—then the organization starts to transform. All the employees understand the direction of the company and begin working that way. Employees must know that the 14 points are a complete system of management, not a passing phase or a new trend. It is up to senior management to keep the focus of all employees on the 14 points. It is up to management to get feedback from all employees and improve the organization. Implementing the 14 points in a piecemeal fashion will never work.

Deming: Use of visible figures only, for management, visible figures only, with little or no consideration of figures that are unknown or unknowable. I may ask people, "Why do you talk about figures that are unknown? If it's unknown, how do you know that it's important?"

Well, let's have a look at some of the unknown and unknowable figures. Very simple!

One of them is the multiplying effect of a happy customer. How much business does a happy customer bring in to you?

Nobody knows. There are conjectures, but nobody knows. What about the multiplying effect of an unhappy customer?

It drives business away. He can be pretty effective. He does his best to protect his friends.

Where are the figures, where are the figures on the multiplying effect of a happy customer and the multiplying effect of an unhappy customer?

I don't see the figures.

Video resources:

Andrew: http://youtu.be/txTIk8PvDVw

Dr. Deming: http://youtu.be/XcWVibi6DEA

15 THE DEMING PRIZE JOURNEY FOR THAI CARBON BLACK

The Deming Prize is one of the highest quality prizes a company can win. To understand how to achieve this, let's follow the journey of one prize winner.

The man

Mr. Subbaraman Srinivasan, BE, MBA, has more than 38 years of industrial experience at Fortune 500 companies and multinational corporations. He is a regular speaker at global CEO forums and other world conferences on quality, productivity, and improvement.

He has been an honorary trade adviser to the Thai Ministry of Commece and is an Institute of Directors graduate member. He was president and director for SEA, and China for Thai Carbon Black PCL, and held the last position of senior executive president and director, global chief of pulp operations for India, SEA and Canada.

Mr. Srinivasan was named the Best CEO in Thailand in 2004. He has led companies to achieve world-class awards such as the Union of Japanese Scientists and Engineers (JUSE) "Deming Prize", the Japan Institute of Plant Maintenance (JIPM) Total Productive Maintenance (TPM)

Excellence Award, Forbes' Best Under a Billion list, for six consecutive years, best employer in Asia and Thailand by Hewitt associates, winner of many National & International awards on Productivity, Quality, HR and Employee relations and significant contributions in CSR.

The Journey

Various initiatives were undertaken to create a strong foundation before embarking on qualifying for the Deming Prize. The building blocks included developing a "shared vision" among all employees, regular communication meetings with all stakeholders, and the use and achievement of different systems and standards.

Thai Carbon Black's (TCB) highly motivated teams with a passion for holistic quality coupled with "can do" attitudes were the most significant contributors in pursuing the Deming philosophy. Facilitation and guidance provided by the Deming Committee and rigorous reviews and auditing molded the organization and employees' effectiveness in taking on the qualitative approach with utmost dedication.

Receipt of the Deming Award is a testament to the commitment and dedication of the teams in meeting these challenges head on, which enabled them to transform the organization into one of "World Class Excellence".

The company took its provision of goods and services from merely customer satisfaction to customer delight. They achieved this in part by driving the organization with process orientation, which caused beneficial results to follow naturally. The company adopted "continuous improvement" through Deming's "Plan, Do, Study, Act" (PDSA) method in all areas of operation, including productivity, quality, cost, delivery, safety, and morale.

Especially in the "Do" phase of Deming's PDSA cycle, it applied the Hoshin Kanri (direction management/policy deployment) system, to elucidate and bolster strategic goals and use the vision and knowledge of all staff and management officers about the direction of the company along with cultivating the means to realize such goals.

Management made all staff and supervisors aware of the cost of poor quality and applied Statistical Quality Control (SQC), Design of Experiments (DOE), and Quality Function Deployment (QFD), also to that end. In doing so, the company is managed by data and led by demonstration, not theory, while also engendering an attitude of respect for all people throughout the organization.

A unique feature that stemmed from the Deming journey was the comprehensive move from a hierarchy to a cross-functional, team-based structure.

Through creation of a shared vision and adoption of all the above methods, the company enhanced stakeholder value across the board, encompassing shareholders, customers, vendors, employees, supervisors, associated learning and other institutions, and the community at large.

16 WHAT IS THE DEMING PRIZE?

A prize devoted to the man.

How was the Deming Prize established?

The late Dr. W. E. Deming (1900–1993), one of the foremost experts of quality control in the United States, was invited to Japan by the Union of Japanese Scientists and Engineers (JUSE) in July 1950. Upon his visit, Dr. Deming lectured his "Eight-Day Course on Quality Control", day after day, at the Auditorium of the Japan Medical Association in Kanda-Surugadai, Tokyo. This was followed by Dr. Deming's "One-Day Course on Quality Control for Top Management," held in Hakone. Through these seminars, Dr. Deming taught the basics of statistical quality control plainly and thoroughly to executives, managers, engineers, and researchers of Japanese industry. His teachings made a deep impression on the participants' minds and provided great impetus to improve quality control in Japan, which was in its infancy.

The transcript of the eight-day course, "Dr. Deming's Lectures on Statistical Control of Quality," was compiled from stenographic records and distributed for a charge. Dr. Deming donated his royalties to JUSE. In appreciation of Dr. Deming's generosity, the late Mr. Kenichi Koyanagi, managing director of JUSE, proposed using the royalties to fund a prize to commemorate Dr. Deming's contribution and friendship in a lasting way and to promote the continued development of quality control in Japan. Upon receiving the proposal, JUSE's board of directors unanimously made a resolution to establish the Deming Prize.

What is the Deming Prize?

The Deming Prize is an annual award presented to an organization that has implemented TQM suitable for its management philosophy, scope/type/scale of business, and management environment. Regardless of the type of business, any organization can apply for the prize under certain conditions – be it public or private, large or small, domestic or overseas, part of or an entire organization.

There is no limit to the number of potential recipients of the prize each year. All organizations that score the passing points or higher upon examination will be awarded the Deming Prize.

What is the TQM Diagnosis?

It is useful to have a third party objectively diagnose the implementation status of TQM and provide recommendations so that the organization can better understand where it stands and what it has to do to promote TQM more effectively.

Established in 1971, the TQM Diagnosis, which is provided by the Deming Prize Examination Committee upon request of an organization, aims to contribute to the further development of that organization's TQM.

TQM Diagnosis by the Deming Prize Committee is recommended for preparing for the Deming Prize challenge or grasping the level of TQM.

Carrying out the TQM diagnosis by the Deming Prize Committee is a mandatory requirement upon application for the Deming Prize/Deming Grand Prize (formerly, the

Japan Quality Medal). In the event that the application is made to prepare for the Deming Prize/Deming Grand Prize challenge, a pre-application consultation will also be carried out by examiners during the on-site TQM diagnosis.

It is also noted that the TQM diagnosis with an aim to prepare for the Deming Prize/Deming Grand Prize will be carried out once, unless otherwise granted by the committee due to changes in application unit, application scope, applicant's organization, etc.

The TQM Diagnosis is not a preliminary Deming Prize/Deming Grand Prize examination. However, since 2000, the connection between the TQM Diagnosis and the Deming Prize/Deming Grand Prize examination strengthened. An organization that receives the TQM Diagnosis cannot apply for the Deming Prize/Deming Grand Prize examination that same year.

TQM Diagnosis procedures:

The purpose of the TQM Diagnosis is to further advance the promotion and practice of effective TQM in organizations under diagnosis. The TQM diagnosis and resulting guidance is provided from an objective viewpoint to organizations at varying stages of TQM advancement, as indicated below. Those organizations that wish to receive the TQM Diagnosis must complete and submit the application form with necessary documents at least three months prior to the desired diagnosis dates. However, no diagnosis will be conducted during the Deming Prize examination period (early July to mid-October).

The Deming Prize Examination Committee conducts the TQM Diagnosis:

To receive a diagnosis and recommendations for the introductory or promotional stage of TQM.

To receive a diagnosis and recommendations for making effective use of the Deming Prize challenge.

To receive a diagnosis and recommendations for

making effective use of the Deming Grand Prize challenge, in lieu of receiving the post-prize review three years after receiving the Deming Prize.

While the details of the diagnosis program will be determined in consultation with the applicant organization, the methods and documents used for the diagnosis follow those for the Deming Prize. As a rule, the diagnosis will be based upon the organization's presentations, the on-site examination, the document review, and questions and answers. The results of the diagnosis will be communicated through a report on the diagnosis findings after the findings of all the examiners who conducted the diagnosis have been compiled. Those companies that wish to receive the TQM Diagnosis should contact the JUSE Secretariat for the Deming Prize Committee:

Additional resources:

The information in this chapter was mainly derived from the following site:

http://www.juse.or.jp/deming_en/

17 CONTINUE LEARNING

If You Enjoyed this Book, You Might Also Like:

Books:
Quality Productivity and Competitive Position, W. Edwards Deming
The New Economics, W. Edwards Deming
Out Of The Crisis, W. Edwards Deming
The Essential Deming: Leadership Principles from the Father of Quality, by W. Edwards Deming
Dr. Deming: The American who Taught the Japanese About Quality, by Rafael Aguayo
Four Days with Dr. Deming: A Strategy for Modern Methods of Management, by William J. Latzko
The Deming Management Method, by Mary Walton
The World of W. Edwards Deming, by Cecelia S. Kilian
Deming: The Way We Knew Him, by Frank Voehl

Websites:
https://www.deming.org
http://curiouscat.com

ABOUT THE AUTHOR

Andrew Stotz, CFA is currently a PhD candidate at the University of Science and Technology of China, Hefei, China. He is the President of CFA Society Thailand and was previously voted Thailand's #1 equity analyst. He runs A. Stotz Investment Research, which provides stock portfolio recommendations across every market in Asia. He has been a university lecturer for 21 years and is co-founder of CoffeeWORKS Co. Ltd., Thailand's leading specialty coffee roaster, and Jcademy.com, an innovative online learning website.

Andrew studied with Dr. Deming on two different occasions when he worked as a supervisor at Pepsi-Cola in Los Angeles and has been studying and applying Dr. Deming's principles in his own businesses and personal life for the last 25 years.

75106275R00059